TALES OF WONDER

LiTTLE TiGER

LONDON

Little Tiger
An imprint of Little Tiger Press Limited
1 Coda Studios, 189 Munster Road, London SW6 6AW
Imported into the EEA by Penguin Random House Ireland,
Morrison Chambers, 32 Nassau Street, Dublin D02 YH68
www.littletiger.co.uk
First published as *Myths and Legends* and *Festivals and Celebrations* 2017
This edition published 2023

A CIP catalogue record for this book is available from the British Library
All rights reserved • Printed in China
ISBN: 978-1-83891-500-1 • CPB/2800/2257/0922
10 9 8 7 6 5 4 3 2 1

FSC
www.fsc.org
MIX
Paper from
responsible sources
FSC® C017606

The Forest Stewardship Council® (FSC®) is an international,
non-governmental organisation dedicated to promoting responsible
management of the world's forests. FSC® operates a system of forest
certification and product labelling that allows consumers to identify
wood and wood-based products from well-managed forests and
other controlled sources.

For more information about the FSC®,
please visit their website at www.fsc.org

TALES OF WONDER

Written by
Sandra Lawrence

Illustrated by
**Jane Newland and
Emma Trithart**

CONTENTS

WELCOME TO OUR MAGICAL, MYSTERIOUS WORLD...

People have always told stories and joined together to mark special occasions like birthdays and weddings. Sometimes the merrymaking bubbles up even further into festivals everyone can enjoy, and some stories become part of our cultural history.

Myths are stories people used to tell to explain things they didn't understand about nature or the world around them. Legends may once have been based on truth but over time have become fabulous fantasies instead.

This book takes a journey around the world, discovering tales from different societies and cultures and showcasing the brightest, most beautiful festivals on the planet.

Zeus (Greek)

Quetzalcoatl (Aztec)

GODS

GOOD GODS

Athena is the Greek goddess of wisdom but also of warfare. Just like people, very few of the deities in ancient tales are all good or all bad. You just don't want to meet a good god having a bad day!

Athena (Greek)

Brigid is the Celtic goddess of poetry, healing and fire. When the Christians came to Ireland, they adopted her and made Brigid a saint!

The feathered serpent god, Quetzalcoatl, from Aztec mythology, is not just the god of creation, wind and farming – he alsxo gave humans chocolate!

Thor, the Norse god of thunder, is not the brightest but he is incredibly loyal, bravely defending Asgard (the realm of the gods) and his friends and family.

Hindu god Vishnu is the protector of the universe. He is believed to return to Earth in troubled times to restore its balance.

8

Thor (Norse)

Vishnu (Hindu)

Odin (Norse)

Brigid (Celtic)

DIVINE TOOLS

Many gods use magical weapons to channel their power. Zeus uses thunder and lightning to strike his enemies.

The Dagda is the Irish god of life, death and feasting. His club can kill nine men with one blow, but can also return people to life.

Dagda (Irish)

9

Odin's magical spear is called Gungnir, meaning 'swaying one'. Made by the dwarfs, Gungnir is perfectly balanced so it will hit any target, no matter who throws it.

HOLY TECHNOLOGY

The Greek god Hermes, known as Mercury in Roman mythology, carries a staff called a caduceus. It was used by the messenger of the gods to bring about peace or slumber.

The giant Thrym stole Thor's hammer from Asgard and would only
return it if he could marry the goddess, Freya. When she refused,
Thor dressed up in a wedding gown to trick the giant. As Thrym
removed his new wife's veil, he discovered the bearded Norse god,
who proceeded to slay the giant and reclaim his hammer.

STORIES ABOUT THE GODS

PANDORA'S BOX
BE CAREFUL WHAT YOU OPEN...

In Greek mythology, the gods were so angry that Prometheus had stolen their fire to give to humans, they decided to punish mankind.

They made the first woman, Pandora, and gave her gifts of beauty, charm and talent... as well as an insatiable curiosity...

Pandora was given a mysterious box and told never to open it but she disobeyed, letting out all the evils of the world, and leaving behind just one small quality – **hope.**

SHIVA AND GANESHA

When Ganesha, son of the Hindu god Shiva, refused to let his
father in at home, Shiva chopped off his head in a fit of rage!
Parvati, the boy's mother, ordered Shiva to find his son a new head.
He returned with one from the first animal he saw facing north –
a baby elephant!

IT'S A GOD-EAT-GOD WORLD

The king of the Titans, Kronos, swallowed his children as soon as
they were born after hearing a prophecy that one of them would kill
him. His wife, Rhea, hid her last son, Zeus, giving Kronos a stone to
eat instead.

Zeus later returned to Mount Olympus, disguised as a cupbearer.
He gave a potion to the unsuspecting Kronos, making him
violently sick. Kronos' other children, the pantheon of
Greek gods, were finally set free.

BANISHING THE BAD

CRAZY COLOURS

Holi must be the most colourful festival in the world! Indian and Nepalese people rejoice in the victory of good over evil, and springtime over winter, by gathering in the streets and throwing coloured powders, paint and water at each other.

No one escapes – friends or strangers, young or old, rich or poor – everyone gets pelted with colour whilst noise and laughter fill the air. Some people carry giant water guns, and others fill balloons with coloured water to enjoy a massive rainbow-tinged water fight.

BOO!

Villagers in Mohács, Hungary, dress up in horned masks and giant shaggy cloaks to scare harsh winters away. This dates back to a time when they dressed as monsters to frighten an invading army.

TRICKSTERS
NOW YOU SEE THEM...

Tricksters appear in many legends. These cunning characters love to cause chaos.

Norse god Loki is a sweet-talking shapeshifter, who was imprisoned by the other gods after arranging the death of Baldr, the god of joy.

It is said that one day Loki will break free to face the Norse gods in one final battle.

The trickster Spider-god Anansi appears in many Ghanaian and Caribbean folktales. He is generally good and wise, using his cunning against enemies who are stronger than him. Stories of Anansi are meant to give humans hope that they can overcome bad situations too.

SUPERSTITIONS

GREAT BALLS OF FIRE!

Thousands of Scottish people take to the streets for their New Year celebration, Hogmanay. In the small village of Stonehaven, people parade through the streets, whirling balls of fire around. According to tradition, these burn away last year's evil spirits so that new, good spirits can begin their work.

WISHING UPON A BONFIRE...

The ancient Iranian fire festival Chaharshanbe Suri, or 'Red Wednesday', takes place on the last Wednesday before Nowruz (New Year). People jump over bonfires to chase away bad luck and illness, and children run through the streets in disguise, banging pots and pans with spoons, and asking for treats, as it is believed that wishes come true on that night.

IN WITH THE NEW...

In some parts of southern Italy people still celebrate New Year by throwing their old furniture, pots and pans out of windows to show they are letting go of unhappiness in preparation for the coming year.

Thailand's Songkran festival washes away sins and bad luck. Young people gently pour water over the palms of their elders' hands – then start on each other, resulting in a massive water fight in the streets!

GOOD LUCK

FIRECRACKERS AND
LUCKY DRAGONS

At New Year, Chinese people prepare for good fortune by cleaning their homes and filling their windows with lanterns and beautiful paper-cuts. Decorations, clothes and even the envelopes of money exchanged as gifts are usually in the luckiest colour of all: red.

Families eat a special dinner, and afterwards make as much noise as possible to scare away evil spirits with fireworks, or by burning bamboo sticks – an early form of firecracker. Dancers parade in long dragon puppets, as these are lucky creatures. At night, lamps are lit inside the bodies so that they glow as though they're on fire.

SHAMROCKS AND LEPRECHAUNS

Wherever Irish people are in the world, they love to celebrate their patron saint, Patrick. In Ireland his day is a national holiday. Lots of traditional folk music is played and some cities hold huge parades. People carry lucky shamrocks (four-leaf clovers) and everyone wears as much green as possible.

In Chicago in the USA, they even dye the water in the river bright green! When this tradition began in 1962, it could take up to a month for the river to return to its normal colour, but nowadays the eco-friendly dye only lasts for a few hours. People take cruises along the river as part of the celebrations.

RELIGIOUS PRACTICES AND CELEBRATIONS

LOVE'S LIGHT

The Ramayana is the ancient Indian myth of Prince Rama's search for his lost princess, Sita.

Sita was kidnapped by the 10-headed, 20-armed demon Ravana, who carried a magic blessing so no human, god or spirit could kill him.

Rama and his brother Lakshmana went through many adventures together in search of Sita. Finally, they amassed an army of monkeys and bears and returned the princess to her prince.

HOLIDAY SEASONS

Children in many countries leave stockings, pillowcases and even shoes for Father Christmas to fill with gifts and sweets on Christmas Eve. In some countries, naughty children find a gift of coal on Christmas morning!

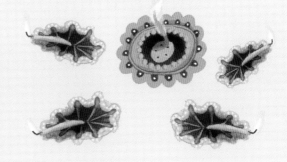

Diwali, the ancient Hindu festival of lights, celebrates the victory of light over darkness and good over evil. People dress in their best clothes, light *diyas* (small lamps and candles), share sweets and exchange gifts.

During Hanukkah, Jewish people commemorate a miracle in which a jar of oil lasted for eight days. They light a candelabra called a menorah and eat rich, oil-based foods, such as potato latkes and doughnuts.

21

WASSAIL

Twelfth Night is traditionally the last day of Christmas revelries. In England, the 'Holly Man' 'wassails' (toasts) everybody outside the Globe Theatre in London.

'Mummers' dress up and perform plays and people hold hands in a chain to dance a farandole.

FOLKLORE AND STORYTELLING

MYTHICAL REALMS

People have always imagined lost civilisations filled with huge riches, magic and beauty...

In the mountains of South America lies the legend of El Dorado, a city supposedly made of pure gold.

The philosopher Plato famously made up the underwater city of Atlantis, but people still believed it existed and it even appears on some early maps!

PULLING STRINGS

Whether a simple face made from a sock, or elaborate marionettes with lots of strings, people have been using puppets to tell stories for more than 3,000 years.

Tehran, in Iran, invites puppeteers from around the world to perform at a giant festival of puppetry. In the opening parade there are puppets so big the puppeteers have to wear them!

DON'T LOSE YOUR HEAD!

One of the best bits of the colourful festival of El Pilar, in Zaragoza, Spain, is the parade of the 'giants and big heads' (*gigantes y cabezudos*). These huge, costumed puppets are made of papier mâché and are worn by people who operate them from inside.

QUESTS AND BRAVERY

JASON AND THE GOLDEN FLEECE

Jason, the rightful king of Thessaly, Greece, was sent by his usurping uncle Pelias to find the legendary golden ram's fleece, which was guarded by fire-breathing bulls and a fearsome dragon. If he succeeded, Pelias would let Jason reclaim his throne.

Jason and his men (the Argonauts) set sail, encountering terrifying storms, clashing rocks, a group of six-armed giants, fire-breathing oxen, vicious half-human birds called harpies, a magical army born from dragons' teeth and even a robot-like creature, called Talos!

Jason eventually returned with the fleece to be crowned king. But this was not the end of his adventures for there are many more legends of Jason, the Argonauts and their families.

24

QUEST FOR THE HOLY GRAIL

The Grail is a religious artefact with great powers of regeneration and healing. It was believed to have been kept in a strange castle in the middle of mysterious wastelands. Many of King Arthur's knights set out to search for it.

The vessel could only be found by the purest of heart. Although the knights were brave and bold, most were not considered worthy. Eventually, Sir Galahad passed all the tests – saving Sir Percival from 20 enemies and rescuing many maidens in distress. He was allowed to take the Grail to the isle of Sarras, where it was lifted to heaven, away from human failings.

MYTHICAL JOURNEYS

THE SEVEN STORIES OF SINBAD

In the famous Middle Eastern folktale Sinbad the Sailor, a poor porter goes to the house of a rich merchant. This merchant, Sinbad, tells him stories of his life as a young man at sea.

Each voyage Sinbad takes is more fantastical than the last. He encounters monsters, kings and giants, but also finds fabulous lands and sumptuous wealth. He is often shipwrecked and in peril but uses cunning to succeed.

In the second of the seven stories, a shipwrecked Sinbad ties himself to the talons of a giant bird of prey called a *roc* in order to escape. The bird unwittingly flies him to its nest in a valley filled with diamonds. Eventually, he is rescued by some merchants and Sinbad returns home a very rich man indeed!

ANIMAL ADVENTURES

Legend tells of two Hungarian princes who chased
a strange deer with glittering antlers. They followed
the stag to distant lands before it disappeared into
a lake. The brothers built a temple on the land and
married two local princesses. It is said their children
founded two nations – the Huns and the Magyars.

In Maori legend, Maui-mua searches for his missing
sister, Hina-uri. He travels long distances, breaking
through the heavens and even turning himself into a
bird to find her.

TODAY'S JOURNEYS

SUNNY DAYS

The mysterious builders of Stonehenge, an ancient English monument, were skilled astronomers. They aligned the rocks so the Sun would rise over a single stone at dawn on midsummer morning. Many visitors still come to see it.

ROMA RHYTHMS

Each May, Romani people from across Europe come together in the small fishing village of Saintes-Maries-de-la-Mer in France. They meet with the *gardians*, or Camargue cowboys, famous for their white horses. Together they celebrate Saint Sara, their patron saint.

Music floats through tall, waving marsh grasses, as revellers show off their riding skills, dance the flamenco and carry a statue of Saint Sara into the waves for her annual visit to the seaside.

A LOAD OF HOT AIR

October's crisp, still mornings are perfect for hot air ballooning. In Albuquerque, USA, nearly 600 hot air balloons gather for a spectacular flight into clear blue skies.

The hot air balloons are all shapes and sizes and every colour of the rainbow. You might see a scarecrow, a boot, a pirate ship or even an alien! At night they take flight again. The pilots all fire their burners at the same time, softly lighting up the darkness together.

HEROES

MEET THE HEROES

English outlaw Robin Hood fought injustice, stealing from the rich to give to the poor.

Finn MacCool was an Irish hunter-warrior, who some legends claim created the Giants' Causeway in Ireland.

Sun Wukong was a Chinese demon who was jailed for five centuries by the Buddha for bad behaviour. When freed, he was sent to protect a pilgrim on a long journey where he proved himself a hero after all.

Japanese legend Kintaro was super-strong, even as a child. He was brought up in the mountains by a forest witch and there are many tales of his childhood battles with monsters and demons.

Sun Wukong

Robin Hood　　　*Finn MacCool*　　　*Kintaro*

LIGHT YOUR WHITE CANDLES, ST LUCIA

Each year, on 13th December,
Scandinavian towns elect a girl
to play Saint Lucia, who brought
food and drink to refugees hiding
in catacombs (underground
cemeteries) in ancient times.
She wore a wreath of candles
to light her way, so that she
could carry as much food as
possible in her arms.

During the grand procession, songs
are sung to mark Advent, and to
celebrate keeping the light alive
during the dark winter months.
Boys wear cone-shaped hats
decorated with stars.

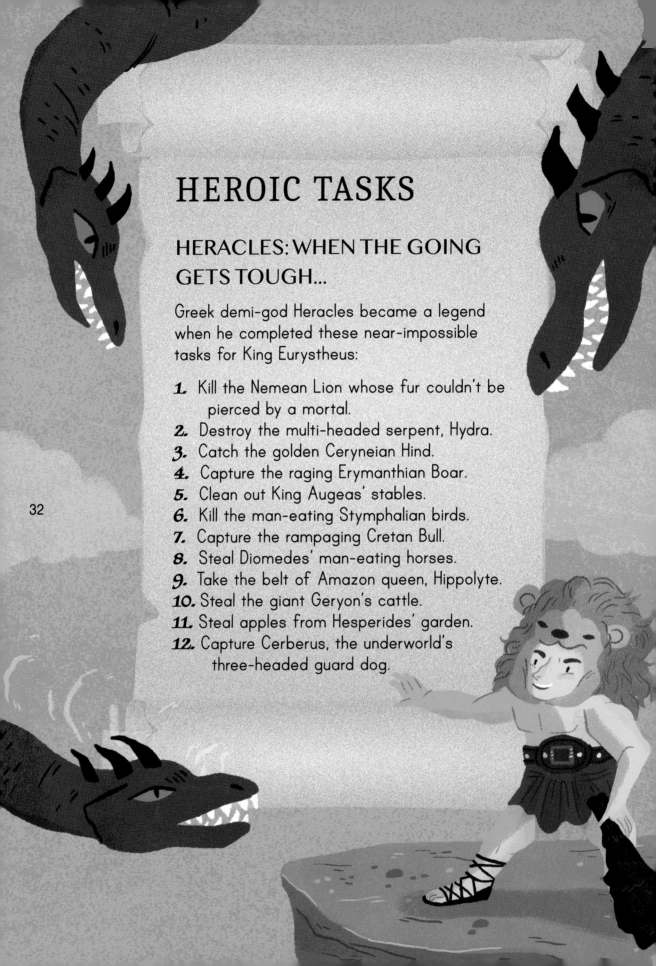

HEROIC TASKS

HERACLES: WHEN THE GOING GETS TOUGH...

Greek demi-god Heracles became a legend when he completed these near-impossible tasks for King Eurystheus:

1. Kill the Nemean Lion whose fur couldn't be pierced by a mortal.
2. Destroy the multi-headed serpent, Hydra.
3. Catch the golden Ceryneian Hind.
4. Capture the raging Erymanthian Boar.
5. Clean out King Augeas' stables.
6. Kill the man-eating Stymphalian birds.
7. Capture the rampaging Cretan Bull.
8. Steal Diomedes' man-eating horses.
9. Take the belt of Amazon queen, Hippolyte.
10. Steal the giant Geryon's cattle.
11. Steal apples from Hesperides' garden.
12. Capture Cerberus, the underworld's three-headed guard dog.

KING ARTHUR
THE ONCE AND FUTURE KING

Nobody knows if Arthur, the legendary king of the Britons, ever existed, but there are lots of tales about the quests of Arthur and his knights of the Round Table.

As a young man, Arthur pulled an immovable sword from a stone, proving he was England's rightful king. Was this his magical sword Excalibur, or did the Lady of the Lake rise from the lake depths to give Arthur Excalibur after he'd been crowned?

The legend goes that Arthur never really died but instead lies asleep in Avalon, waiting for Britain to truly need him.

THE ANTI-HEROES

MWAHAHAHA... IT'S THE BAD GUYS!

The Caribbean spirit of death, Baron Samedi, lurks on the crossroad between life and death, waiting to dig your grave. But, on the plus side, he will make sure you don't turn into a zombie!

Medusa can turn a man to stone with one look and Set is the god of chaos and destruction – so don't get on the wrong side of him!

However, not all baddies are totally evil. Baba Yaga, for example, will try to eat passers-by but will also tell the truth if asked nicely.

ID: **Baba Yaga**

Russian

Central Police Department

ID: **Baron Samedi**

Haitian

Central Police Department

ID: **Medusa**

Ancient Greek

Central Police Department

ID: **Set**

Egyptian

Central Police Department

6.2"
6.0"
5.10"
5.8"
5.6"
5.4"

NASTY MYTHOLOGICAL BEASTS

According to German folklore, the shape-changing Alp sits on the chests of sleepers until they wake up in a breathless terror.

The Greek Chimera is a terrifying mix of a lion's head and body, a goat's head and a serpent for a tail. Greek hero Bellerophon needed the help of winged horse Pegasus to attack both heads and kill the Chimera.

Mizuchi are water spirits in the form of wingless dragons. Japanese legend tells of one emperor sending human sacrifices to the Mizuchi after angering them by building a dam.

VICTORY!

THESEUS: HIGHLY-STRUNG HEROICS

King Minos of Crete had a problem: a human-eating beast known as the Minotaur. Minos locked the Minotaur in a labyrinth, demanding that his neighbour, King Aegeus, send 14 young people each year to feed the monster.

Eventually King Aegeus' son, Theseus, vowed to kill the Minotaur and end the annual bloodshed. On arriving in Crete, Theseus met King Minos' daughter, Ariadne, who wanted to leave her kingdom.

GOOD TRIUMPHS OVER EVIL

Hindu demon-king Mahishasura thought he was invincible because he could only be killed by a woman and he didn't believe one would be capable of such a feat.

In exchange for safe passage, she gave Theseus a ball of string, so he could find his way out of the impossible maze.

Theseus found and killed the monster, and led the sacrifices back to safety using Ariadne's thread. He then kept his promise to take Ariadne away with him.

When he began to terrorise both humans and gods, the great gods Brahma, Vishnu and Shiva created Durga, a many-armed, fearsome female warrior.

Mahishasura and his demons attacked her, but Durga, filled with the good of the world, fought back and finally chopped his head off.

FESTIVALS FOR GRATITUDE

WHEN ALL IS SAFELY GATHERED IN

Many communities across the world celebrate harvest-time. In the UK, people bring fruit and vegetables to church for a big display at their Harvest Festival. The centrepiece is often a 'corn-dolly', traditionally made from the season's last sheaf of wheat or corn.

THANKSGIVING

In the USA, Thanksgiving is a time for families to enjoy parades, sports and food such as sweet potatoes, cornbread, pumpkin pie and turkey. Every year, though, one turkey is allowed to go free. The president 'pardons' the bird, which goes to live in a zoo or on a farm.

HOPPY EASTER

Easter is a popular spring festival, and Easter eggs are an ancient symbol of new life. In Germany and the UK, people roll hard-boiled eggs down hills, competing to see whose egg goes the furthest.

Modern Easter eggs are usually made from chocolate but many countries still paint hens' eggs in bright colours. In Ukraine, traditional *pysanky* (eggs) are decorated with wax patterns before being dyed.

HONOURING LOST LOVED ONES

DAY OF THE DEAD

On the *Día de los Muertos* or 'Day of the Dead', Mexican people gather to remember loved ones who are no longer with them.

They build cheery shrines decorated with marigold flowers, treats and shiny trinkets. Brightly coloured sugar skulls and bones are popular. At night people dress up in fiesta clothes, paint their faces to look like skulls and dance to celebrate the lives of the dead.

WINTER WONDERS

At the *Eyo* festival in Lagos, Nigeria, Yoruba people dress in white, while masked dancers leap and spin in honour of departed souls.

Shetland Islanders celebrate their Viking roots once a year at *Up Helly Aa*, a festival of fire. Close to 1,000 people take part in torch processions, then throw the flares into a model of a Viking longship.

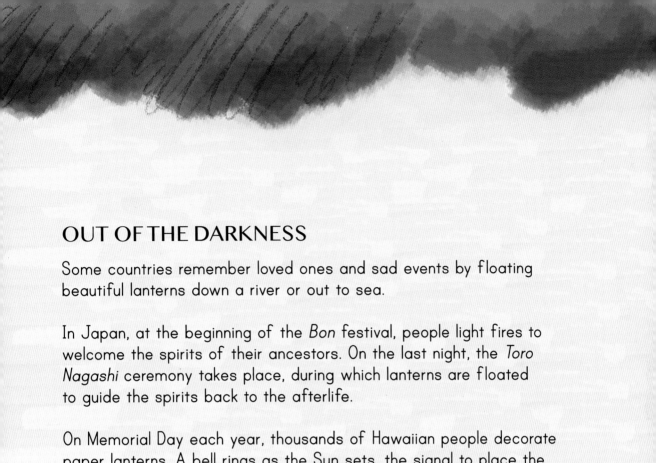

OUT OF THE DARKNESS

Some countries remember loved ones and sad events by floating beautiful lanterns down a river or out to sea.

In Japan, at the beginning of the *Bon* festival, people light fires to welcome the spirits of their ancestors. On the last night, the *Toro Nagashi* ceremony takes place, during which lanterns are floated to guide the spirits back to the afterlife.

On Memorial Day each year, thousands of Hawaiian people decorate paper lanterns. A bell rings as the Sun sets, the signal to place the lights gently onto the water and watch them float away into the Pacific Ocean.

CARNIVALS

LET THE GOOD TIMES ROLL...

New Orleans in the USA is famous for its annual carnival, Mardi Gras (which means 'Fat Tuesday' in French). This magical celebration of music, food and culture sees colourful parade floats fill the city streets.

A VENETIAN MASQUERADE

At Italy's Carnival of Venice, people wear mysterious masks and elaborate costumes that sparkle with beads and golden lace.

Revellers parade the streets, listen to music in the city squares and ride in gondolas. At night they wear cloaks and hats to attend glamorous moonlit parties.

ALOHA HONOLULU!

In memory of their last king, Hawaiians celebrate spring with the Merrie Monarch Festival. This week of dancing, music and storytelling includes ancient 'hula' dance competitions. The most important honour goes to the female winner, who is crowned Miss Aloha Hula.

DANCING 'TIL DAWN

Brazil's Rio de Janeiro has the world's biggest street carnival. Over two million people watch huge parades of floats, music and dance each day.

Dancers practise all year to *batucada* music and skilled costume-makers craft amazing outfits with sequins and feathers.

THE COMMUNITY COMING TOGETHER

MAY DAY

The first day of May has been celebrated throughout the Northern Hemisphere for centuries. In some English villages, they still elect a 'May Queen' and children dance around maypoles.

MIDSUMMER MADNESS

Sweden's summer is short but intense. At *midsommar* the Sun sets very late and in some northern areas there is no sunset!

People rejoice in this brief time, picnicking among the trees and wearing flower garlands, called *krans*, to bring good luck. They eat summer berries, dance around a leaf-covered pole and play party games.

TARRAGONA TOWERS

Catalonia in Spain is the home of the *castell*, or 'human tower'.

Originating in Tarragona, teams of people compete to build and successfully dismantle the highest towers.

The biggest, burliest *castellers* form the *pinya*, or 'base', the nimbler ones slowly climb up to create storeys, with the smallest, lightest folk on top.

Sometimes there can be up to 10 layers of people!

45

HISTORICAL CELEBRATIONS

FRIGHT NIGHT

Many countries celebrate All Hallows' Eve, when the spirits are said to walk among us. French people would historically leave dishes of milk for them and Italians left entire meals. Spanish bakers still make almond pastries called 'bones of the holy'.

'Trick or treating' began in Scotland and Ireland. People would go from house to house in disguises asking for small gifts. If refused they would play pranks on the householders. These 'guisers' carried hollowed-out turnips with candles inside to light their way. When the tradition spread to North America, pumpkins were used instead.

46

REMEMBER, REMEMBER, THE FIFTH OF NOVEMBER!

Over 400 years ago, a plot to blow up the British Houses of Parliament ended with the capture and deaths of the conspirators.

It was Guy Fawkes' job to light the fuse, so British people now call 5th November 'Guy Fawkes Night'. They hold fireworks displays and light bonfires, with a 'Guy' of old clothes stuffed with straw placed on top.

FREEDOM AND FIREWORKS

Each year on 4th July, the USA celebrates the original 13 colonies gaining their independence from the British Empire.

People attend baseball games, family barbecues, fairs and parades. Children ride on homemade floats, while cheerleaders and baton-twirlers entertain the crowds with their skills. At night, there are spectacular fireworks displays!

FOOD

FIGHT! FIGHT!

Buñol, Spain, is the home of *La Tomatina*, the world's biggest food fight. Every August hundreds of people pelt each other with squashed tomatoes. Some wear swimming masks and snorkels to see and breathe!

It may look very messy but after the fight, enormous water cannons immediately clear the streets. The acid in the tomatoes actually leaves the houses cleaner than they were before.

48

MONSTERS OF THE DEEP

There are lots of different stories about how the Chinese *Tuen Ng*, or 'Dragon Boat Festival', came about, but most people agree that the best parts are the food, drink and dragon boat racing.

People prepare *zongzi* (sticky rice balls in bamboo leaves). They eat some and drop the rest into the river. One popular legend holds that this is done so the fish won't eat the body of an ancient poet!

RADISH REVOLUTION

The city of Oaxaca in Mexico has a long tradition of wood-carving, but once a year they turn their skills to giant radishes! It's thought the tradition began one year when the region had too many.

Over 200 years later, radishes are deliberately left in the ground to grow as large as possible, then transformed by carvers into strange scenes and figures. There are prizes for the best entries.

Everybody wants to see the radishes, and huge queues form to view the sculptures before they begin to wilt.

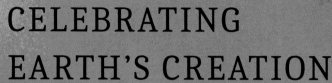

CELEBRATING EARTH'S CREATION

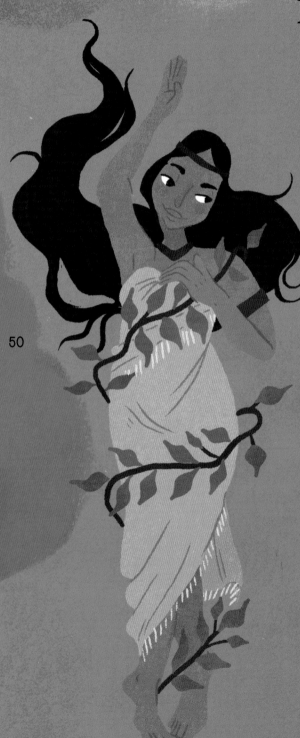

'IN THE BEGINNING...'

There are as many myths about the Native American spirit Sky Woman as there are tribes. Most agree that she fell to Earth from the sky and was helped on her way down by Earth's birds and animals.

Sky Woman gave birth to twins, the Good and the Evil Spirit. They created the world in perfect balance, ensuring there was good and evil in everything.

In the Australian indigenous myth, the world was once a dark, flat nothing with the Sun, Moon, stars and life asleep under the surface.

At creation, the eternal ancestors burst through the Earth's crust. First came the Sun, followed by the other spirits, who lived together in Dreamtime, creating landscapes and creatures as they went.

MINI STORIES: MORE BEGINNINGS

God Mbombo of Africa's Kuba kingdom was alone in a great sea. Suddenly he was violently sick, expelling the Sun, the Moon and stars! The heat from the Sun evaporated the water, making land. Mbombo then vomited once more to produce animals and people.

Hindu mythology tells of a giant turtle, called Akupara, carrying the world, borne by elephants, on his back. He's not alone! The Chinese and Native Americans also have stories of a cosmic turtle holding up the heavens.

THE WEATHER

SOLAR FLAIR

To our ancestors, the Sun represented not just warmth and light but also health for their animals and growth for their crops. In several mythologies, gods would move the Sun across the sky during a day.

The Egyptian Sun god, Ra, carried it in two sky-ships called solar barques, one for day (called Madjet), the other for night (called Semektet). The serpent Apophis, god of chaos, always tried to stop Ra but every morning Ra won out and the Sun rose again.

The Greeks had Helios, a handsome Titan, driving the Sun across the sky in a golden chariot pulled by four fire-spitting horses.

But poor Tsohanoai, the Navajo Native American Sun god, was given no transport at all! He would trudge across the sky with the Sun on his back, hanging it on a peg at the day's end before beginning again the next morning.

THUNDER AND LIGHTNING

The crash and flash of violent storms terrified our ancestors.
To each culture, the answer to the dramatic weather was obvious...

The mythological Lightning Bird of South Africa can summon thunder
and lightning by beating its wings and striking its talons.

In Chinese mythology, Dian Mu produces lightning by flashing mirrors
into the sky. Her husband, Lei Gong, creates thunder with a mallet
and drum, punishing evil people with his chisel. Lightning flashes
before the thunder so that Lei Gong can check he is punishing the
right person before he strikes!

FROSTY'S BIG BROTHERS

Many countries believe that snow should be celebrated.
Harbin, in China, gets so cold in the winter that snow
and ice can be carved into fantastical sculptures.
People come from all over the world to see who
can create the best carvings in a glowing,
frozen city of ice and snow.

Some of the palaces, temples,
figures and famous places
are multi-coloured; others
are clear, like glass.

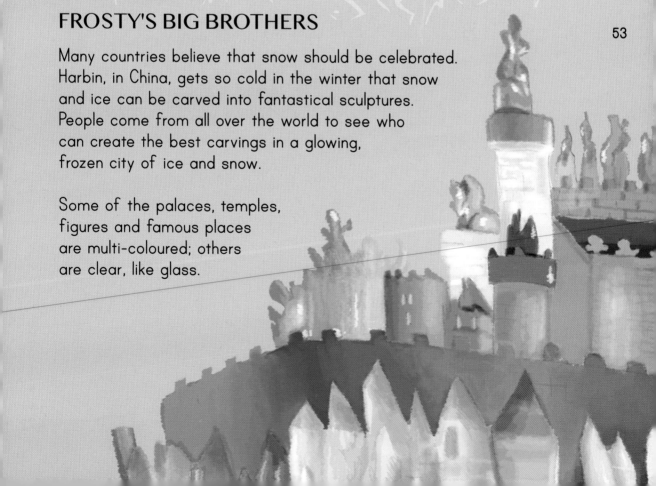

PLANT LIFE

LOVE BLOSSOMS

When Hawaiian goddess Pele saw handsome warrior Ohia, she was smitten, but Ohia already loved a local girl, Lehua. Pele was furious – how dare a mortal turn down a goddess? In anger, she turned Ohia into a twisted, ugly, old tree for rejecting her.

Lehua was heartbroken. Though the other gods pitied her, they could not reverse Pele's powerful magic, so they turned her into a beautiful flower on Ohia's tree so they could be together forever.

It is said that you should never pick a red lehua blossom, as the sky will fill with the lovers' tears.

THE TREE OF LIFE

Many cultures, from the Middle East to South America, have the Tree of Life at the centre of their mythology. The roots represent the underworld, the trunk and branches are the Earth and the green leaves and twigs at the top represent the realm of the gods.

In Norse mythology, Yggdrasil is an enormous ash tree that grows through the three flat discs that make up the world. Its roots are constantly being chewed by a dragon called Nidhogg, who sends insulting messages to an eagle living in the top branches via Ratatoskr, a squirrel who runs up and down the trunk.

BLOOMING BEAUTIFUL

In Japan, *hanami*, or 'flower-viewing', is so important that TV weather forecasters tell people the best times to see the cherry blossoms or *sakura*.

People dress up to walk under the delicate flowers and enjoy picnics, remembering that life, like the petals' time, is short and should be enjoyed.

NATURAL PHENOMENA

SEASONAL TALES

The Ancient Greeks explained the changing seasons with the tale of Hades, god of the underworld, kidnapping the beautiful Persephone.

Her mother Demeter, the harvest goddess, searched for nine days for her daughter before she realised what had happened and begged Hades to return her. He refused, saying that she had eaten four underworld pomegranate seeds so was bound to his kingdom forever.

Eventually, a deal was reached and Persephone was allowed to return to Earth for eight months of the year, bringing with her new life and the spring. For the other four months, she returns to live underground with Hades and winter stalks the land above.

OTHER NATURAL PHENOMENA

How do you explain something as magical as the Aurora Borealis?
In Finnish folklore, the Revontulet, or 'Fox Fire', is caused by a magical
fox sweeping his tail across the snow, swishing it into the sky.

Meanwhile, New Zealand's Te Arawa tribe say the boiling geysers
across the North Island are caused by fire demons, summoned
many years ago, to save the life of a dying Maori priest.

ALL THE YEAR LONG

SPRING FLINGS

Walpurgisnacht is the night when, according to ancient folklore, witches were thought to dance on Brocken Mountain in Harz, Germany, while awaiting the arrival of spring. Nowadays, people dress up as witches and hold spooky parties to celebrate.

Sandfest is a sand sculpture festival in Texas, but they happen all around the world. People compete to make unusual, interesting and often extremely intricate designs out of sand, which eventually disappear in the wind and rain.

KEEPING THE SUN GOD SWEET

In the Southern Hemisphere, June is a winter month. In Cusco, Peru, the festival of *Inti Raymi* re-enacts ancient Incan rituals honouring the sun god, Inti, at midwinter on the shortest day of the year.

Sapa Inca, the ancient emperor, and his queen, Mama Occlo, are carried on golden thrones to a ruined fortress, followed by people dressed as pumas, snakes and condors. A great spectacle in the arena later spills into merrymaking in the streets.

A CORNUCOPIA OF AUTUMN DELIGHTS

The ancient Horn Dance at Abbots Bromley in England dates back to the Middle Ages. Six 'deer men' carry reindeer antlers (carbon dated at over 900 years old), and travel a 16km (10mi) circuit, dancing as they go.

As winter approaches in Europe, cattle and sheep are brought back from high pastures to lower-level valleys. The animals are decked in ribbons, flowers and bells for the Transhumance festival, which celebrates their safe homecoming.

60

RACING RUDOLPH

The Nenets people of Siberia are nomadic: instead of living in one place, they follow their reindeer herds, searching for pasture. Once a year, they get together for Reindeer Herder's Day to celebrate their precious animals. The sleds are usually heavily laden with equipment but with all the pots and pans removed and just one driver to pull, the reindeer can travel very fast indeed!

GLOSSARY

Alphorn ~ a German horn instrument

Ancestors ~ relatives who lived in the past

Aurora Borealis ~ the Northern Lights

Aztecs ~ an ancient people who originated in Mexico

Celtic ~ an ancient language and group of people who originated in Central Europe and spread north, eventually gaining a stronghold in Great Britain where they remained

Commemorate ~ to mark or celebrate someone or something

Community ~ a group of people who live in the same area and have beliefs or ways of life in common

Cosmic ~ something that comes from the universe as opposed to Earth

62

Elder ~ a member of a community who is both older in age and well respected

Eternal ~ something that can last forever

Festival ~ a day or period of time when people celebrate something

Fiesta ~ a religious festival

Folklore ~ a set of beliefs, customs and stories held by a community that have been passed down the generations by word of mouth

Fortune ~ good luck

Gondola ~ a long, narrow boat often found on Venice's canals

Inca ~ an ancient people who originated from the South American Andes mountains

Indigenous ~ someone who is native to a certain place

Labyrinth ~ a complicated maze of passages

Longship ~ a long, narrow warship, which is powered by oars and sails

Maori ~ the indigenous people of New Zealand

Maypole ~ a pole that has been decorated with flowers, which people dance around on May Day

Mortal ~ a human being who will not live forever

Navajo ~ a group of people native to Arizona, Utah and New Mexico

Norse ~ an ancient language and group of people originating from Scandinavia

Outlaw ~ a person who has broken the law

Parade ~ a big procession in public

Patron saint ~ a saint who is believed to give help to certain communities or places

Pilgrim ~ a person who journeys to a holy place

Quest a long and difficult search for something

Realm ~ a kingdom

Regeneration ~ the act of being grown again

Revelry ~ a lively celebration

Scandinavia ~ the group name for Denmark, Norway, Sweden, Finland and Iceland

Serpent ~ a large snake

Shapeshifter ~ a mythological being with the ability to change their appearance

Shrine ~ a place of worship with connections to a specific person or object

Stonehenge ~ a prehistoric monument in England

Sugar skull ~ a decorative skull used in Mexican 'Day of the Dead' celebrations

Transhumance festival ~ a festival celebrating the summer months in southern France

Underworld ~ a supernatural world that many religions believe we enter when we die

Vessel ~ a hollow container used to hold liquid

Vikings ~ Scandinavian people who travelled by sea from the 8th to the 11th century

Warrior ~ a brave and skilled soldier